Tending YOUR Garden

Blessing Heaven and Earth

A Book on Abundant Living by
Kim Corden

Tending Your Garden
Blessing Heaven and Earth
by Kim Corden

First Printing May 2013 in the United States of America

ISBN: 978-0-9857942-7-9

Prepared for Publication By Palm Tree Publications
a Division of Palm Tree Productions
www.palmtreeproductions.com
PO BOX 122 | Keller, TX | 76244

The Light Line
A Division of Try Solutions

Unit 30
Moor Park Industrial
Centre
Tolpits Lane
Watford
Hertfordshire
WD18 9SP
United Kingdom
www.thelightline.net

Dedication

This book is dedicated to all the intercessors and
prayer warriors from the beginning of time.
Thank you for the legacy you have left us,
the covering you have given us, and the
ground you have prepared for us to walk on.
In the hidden place you have been found faithful!

"... they made me keeper of the vineyards, but my own vineyard I have not kept."

Song of Songs 1:6

Contents

Part One—The State of Your Garden

Part Two —The Areas in Your Garden

Part Three—The Blessings from Your Garden

Tending Your Garden

What Others
are Saying ...

We have been blessed over many years through our friendship with Kim. With great passion, she throws herself into "pressing on," and walking in whatever "light" God has shined upon her path (Philippians 3:14-16). What follows her is transformation—the embodiment and authority in her life that challenges and encourages others. Her cup truly overflows, not with theory or head-knowledge, but with the wisdom and grace that comes from the Master Himself. If you are "weary and heavy laden," then come and drink from the living waters you will find flowing through Kim's life and through the pages of this book.

———————————————

John Gere
Leadership Team of Succat Hallel House of Prayer
Jerusalem, Israel

Meeting Kim Corden was one of God's divine appointments for us. My wife, two children, and I live in Dubai, and I'm a banker by profession. When I met Kim, we were in dire need of a breakthrough in my career, but more importantly in the health of my daughter who had been diagnosed with a terminal lung disorder.

Kim agreed to take us on as clients. This intercessor soon became our trusted friend, and we now think of her as a close family member we can turn to for prayer, guidance, and learning.

Kim began covering us in prayer, and in less than twelve months, we saw significant breakthrough in my career and our walk with God has become far more intimate. Most significantly, within four months of working with Kim, we were informed by our doctors that my daughter's lung issue was no longer terminal—it was arrested in its tracks. Intercession works!

Harsha Jayatunge
Head of Financial Institution Sales
Southern Gulf, Levant & North Africa Financial Markets
Standard Chartered Bank
Dubai, UAE

Endorsements

Kim Corden is sent of the Lord to disarm hope-lessness and loss of focus to those advancing the kingdom. She carries in her bright rays of hope that ignite faith by releasing words of life and confirmation. Her obedience to His voice and love of the saints compels her in giving good reports of today's promises and that our God is with us in our generation. Kim's rich and deep faith has been a catalyst in my life and ministry.

Kathleen Liska
Alaska, USA

Kim Corden is a passionate lover of Christ. In *Tending Your Garden*, she inspires you to see beyond the natural realm and stirs up the creativity that God has placed inside of you. You will be encouraged to live in harmony with the Author of creation—on earth as it is in heaven.

Diana Modeley
Intercessor
Mauritius

That the subject of intercession is still uncharted territory in application to business is a curiosity to me. My wife and I began to realize the power of intercessory partnership through our own experience, and Kim Corden has been a real part of this experiment in our lives.

While "cause and effect" are not easily linked together in spiritual matters, I can almost literally sense when Kim has engaged heaven on my behalf—sometimes by the extraordinary grace that is evident in certain key meetings. At other times our spontaneous communication tracks exactly along the same theme. In moments when the spiritual battle is intense, my thoughts will go to Kim and I can sense that at some very tangible level, our shields are linked and all that is needed is a quick update, after which the pressure almost always adjusts.

These kind of strategic alliances put us squarely in the middle of Paul's First Century experience (Philemon 1:22, 1 Timothy 2:2). Kim is part of a new paradigm of ministry and business alignment that will gain greater and greater significance as we keep practicing this vital aspect of prayer partnership, the missing ingredient that enables believers to advance in the midst of spiritual roadblocks and enemies.

Lance Wallnau
President, Lance Learning Group
Fort Worth, Texas, USA

Foreword

by Candy Sunderland

This book, *Tending Your Garden,* is just like the exercise in cultivating creativity found in Genesis 2:8: "And the Lord God planted a garden, eastward of Eden and there He put the man whom He had formed." The Lord created this beautiful garden planet for man, and He still intends for us to cultivate, dress, and prune it as we pass our days here on the earth. From the great surface of the earth to the heart of a child, from the tiniest grain of sand to the power brokers of our day … all of the vibrating, life-giving pieces are to be treated the same. Prophesy to them, nurture and adjust them. Calibrate every vibration to the sound of the Lord. He gave us the pattern and the seed to create "on earth as it is in heaven" (Matthew 6:10).

I love intercessors! There are all kinds—prophetic intercessors, apostolic intercessors, pastoral intercessors, evangelistic intercessors … this great army of God moving across the face of the earth is mostly unrecognized and misunderstood. These intercessors are setting the things of the kingdom in place and removing those that restrict kingdom process. I remember in the 90s when pastors were pulling their own hair out over prophets and trying to figure out what to do with whatever these *intercessors* were. Suddenly a myriad of (mostly ladies) arrived on the scene with notebooks chalked full of scripture, vision, prophesy, and snippets of sentences caught from the great information internet of the Spirit. They would say, "Look, will you read all this that God has said to me?"

I was given great grace to sort through and find the patterns and consistencies of the Spirit of God. These budding intercessors were immature and intense, and many times to work with them was like herding cats. But I would always remember Kenneth Hagin talking about the little old ladies that prayed in churches all over Texas. The Lord uses all the pieces. All the pieces have value and a place.

Only now is the maturing of this great army of prayer warriors being realized. By reason of use, the faithful have honed their gift into precision instruments like spiritual drones in the hand of the Lord. The Great Commander is restructuring this earthly realm. Still mostly unknown and not recognized on platforms, this efficient team of "special ops" has emerged.

Foreword

This book, written for the many who are moving into greater assignments, is the training tool to keep the forces healthy and ready. Like oiled and sharpened weapons, they will accomplish the tasks of the King. Jesus said "My yoke is easy and my burden is light" (Matthew 11:30). By learning to trim and nourish our own lives, we leave the weights of past missions and can stay fresh and of great value.

Kim demonstrates these practices and attributes like no one else I know. She is like the beautiful butterfly who travels from person to person, continent to continent, watering and feeding, snipping and washing, pulling and encouraging heavenly life in all she encounters. This book is sure to delight and inspire you. It will fill you with laughter one moment, and in the next take you deep diving into your own process and journey.

Enjoy a cup of tea in the warm sunshine on a garden bench she will provide ... right before you are whisked away for those fast growth and strengthening exercises. Like Cassius Clay she "floats like a butterfly and stings like a bee."

Candy Sunderland
HAPN I State Leader
Alaska, USA

Tending Your Garden

Preface

This book was birthed after a visit to an Intercessory prayer meeting at Catch the Fire Toronto (formerly Toronto Airport Christian Fellowship) in Canada.

A friend and I had arrived the evening before in transit back to London and had one day in Toronto. I had been to TACF several times and was looking forward to returning there. This time everything seemed different. There were no crowds of people. There was hardly anyone around except a few intercessors in a small, cold back-room meeting to pray for the next wave of Revival they believe is coming.

Even though they didn't know us, we were welcomed in to join the meeting. As I walked into the room, I knew my spirit connected immediately to what was happening and I felt a sense of being "at home." I felt I was with a group of remnant warriors stoking the fire in worship on behalf of this church.

As I sat on the sofa worshipping, I heard the whisper of Father God in my ear, "I want you to write a book and the book will be called *Tending your Garden*." I immediately said "Yes, I will write it," but when I started to think about actually writing a book, I felt daunted by the challenge.

Thank goodness for Wendy Walters (Palm Tree Publications) who put my mind at rest and uncomplicated the task that was ahead!

So here in your hands is the tangible evidence of my obedience (as Wendy would say). It is a book to help those who are passionate for God learn how to be a blessing to heaven, but also a blessing to the earth!

May you be challenged and inspired to go higher in God, find a balance in your life, and have a weed-free spiritual garden. If this is the cry of your heart, then this is written for you.

Acknowledgements

I could not have written this book without encouragement and support from so many people. I would like to say a huge thank you to everyone who, in one way or another, has been a part of making this book what it is. I appreciate those who have contributed to the text and have undergirded this project in prayer, and for special friends around the world who persevered to get their thoughts down on paper! I offer some special thanks to:

- My husband, Martin—for your insight and professional printer's eye.
- My family—for giving me the space to be creative.
- Nick Try—for all your help and support from start to finish, for keeping me focused, and for your wise words.
- Wendy K. Walters—my friend and editor.

This project has been a team effort, and I have a fantastic team!

Tending Your Garden

Introduction

I love my life! I am truly blessed! Why? I live in Hertfordshire, a beautiful part of England on the borders of London and the countryside. I have lived in the same house since I was married to Martin thirty-two years ago, and all our children grew up here. Now my grand-children enjoy the home as well.

I am an outdoors type of person. I love the freedom to enjoy nature, walking the dogs around the lakes, and I take great delight when I ride my horse around the fields. It's a wonderful place to commune with God.

I am also blessed because I have been able to use the gifts God gave me to fulfill my purpose of interceding between heaven and earth. In my work I travel around the world. Sitting still for hours is quite a challenge— so I dream, imagine, and get lost in a creative world of ideas and revelation. I often have the most amazing conversations with total strangers that become good friends! While I have travelled on many planes in the natural, I probably travel more in the spirit, and "pop in and out" of places so often that my American friends are now calling me Mary Poppins!

I live in a real word—a natural world—filled with supernatural signs and wonders. I have experiences that only God could orchestrate, with information only God could give me, with favour to get into places that only God could open the door to. I live an amazingly exciting life!

I hope as we walk through this book together you can get a glimpse through the "Kim lens" and enjoy the journey to greater freedom, clarity, and discernment.

Gardening and Intercession

My husband Martin loves gardening. He can spend hours and hours digging up every single weed in the flower beds, removing the dead-heads from the flowers, and pruning and stringing up bushes and plants so that they all get a little bit of sun without getting their leaves and branches tangled up.

He mows the lawn so that you get those lovely straight lines and makes the garden look fabulous. He does a fantastic job that gives everyone pleasure—not just him.

I (on the other hand) as much as I like gardening, tend to take less time to do a similar task. I will miss

2

some of those hidden weeds, probably design a creative way of stringing up bushes and plants with a little less finesse, and when I mow, the lines are usually not straight across the lawn.

Martin is far more methodical when in the garden. I am far more spontaneous. (I do have to confess that I have often pulled up his bulbs and flowers, thinking they were weeds!)

When it comes to tending your garden spiritually, however, I am far more methodical and focused. I love to do my best to tend to my own garden and help others tend to theirs.

Having been involved in intercession for over thirty years in church, across the nations, and now in the business arena, I have learned that you cannot cut corners. I now know that time and preparation before activation is an absolute must. Otherwise, you are an open target for the enemy, and your role as an intercessor is made harder. Without preparation (pruning, weeding, and tending), your focus and discernment are not so sharp.

I am often asked to speak about intercession. So many people feel a call to pray or intercede, but are not sure how to get started, or if they are even qualified to be an intercessor. I have found myself having many opportunities to work with people, and see them released and flowing in the gifts God has placed within them. I have the privilege to watch them soar and almost become invisible as people see less of them and more of God in them.

Others are merely curious about how to increase the effectiveness of their own personal prayer life and more successfully cover their own families or business with prayer. Opportunities to teach and train continue to open up, but rather than write a "how to" book with prayer principles, I first felt compelled to share how I have experienced God and come to know Him so closely. I wanted to teach others how to tend their spiritual garden and live in a fruitful place. It is from this place of abundance that I touch heaven with my prayers and find direction, guidance, and power on the earth.

What do I mean by "tending your garden" spiritually?

Through the following chapters we will look at some of the areas we need to be aware of that can bring us greater clarity, revelation, and discernment. We will also explore areas that can dull, exhaust, and confuse us as we pray and intercede.

I believe God speaks to us in a clear, uncomplicated way. He provided us with direction and revelation that brings breakthrough quickly. If there are no weeds (hindrances) in our spiritual and physical walk, there is no reason not to see the signs, wonders, and miracles we read about in the Bible.

Introduction

As you explore the areas you are responsible to tend to, I encourage you to open your spiritual ears and listen to the Holy Spirit. He will clearly show you your greatest strengths as well as the areas yet to be refined or strengthened.

At the end of each chapter there will be a short contribution from someone whose life demonstrates fruitfulness in that area. This will encourage you as you embark on this wonderful journey of discovery and growth.

So let's get started ...

"Blessed is the man who walks not in the counsel of the ungodly, nor stands in the path of sinners, nor sits in the seat of the scornful; but his delight is in the law of the Lord, and in His law he meditates day and night. **He shall be like a tree planted by the rivers of water, that brings forth its fruit in its season, whose leaf also shall not wither; and whatever he does shall prosper.**"

Psalm 1:1-3 NKJV
Emphasis Added

Part One

The State
of Your Garden

Tending Your Garden

Chapter One

The Fruitful Garden

The smell of a ripe orchard is wonderful. I enjoy picking my own fruit whenever I can, because I can choose the fruit that is just to my liking. A tasty fruit salad made with a variety of colour and texture is so delicious! It speaks of health, goodness, and vitality.

John 15:8 says, "My Father is glorified by this, that you bear much fruit, and so prove to be my disciples."

What does bearing fruit actually mean? It means that your life demonstrates the grace of God—in character and in actions. We can all carry the distinctive fragrance of God, yet each one of us is a unique expression of Him.

Psalm 1:1-3 says, "How blessed is the man who does not walk in the counsel of the wicked, nor stand in the path of sinners, nor sit in the seat of scoffers!

"But his delight is in the law of the Lord, and in His Law he meditates day and night.

"He will be like a tree firmly planted by streams of water, which yields its fruit in its season and its leaf does not wither; and in whatever he does, he prospers."

Through the wonders of modern technology, our shops can stock most fruit all the year round by importing produce from different countries or cultivating it in a controlled environment. Our supermarkets display every sort of fruit, both seasonal fruit from the UK as well as delicious, but very expensive, exotic fruit from far away lands. Wonderful as these are, they don't compare with produce eaten fresh picked straight from the plant.

If you take a tour around a well-tended orchard, you will see the results of the farmer's loving care for his crop. You will notice that the trees have been pruned to concentrate the growth into strong healthy branches, and the number of fruits on those branches have been limited to improve their quality.

Some years ago I visited the Garden of Gethsemane in Jerusalem with some friends, and I saw pruning in action. Despite the small number of olive trees in this historic garden, it seemed the old gardener was pruning the olive trees right back, cutting off loads of branches. He planted some of the cuttings into little pots, and as he started to talk to us, he gave us each one as a gift. I left the garden with history in my hands!

My little cutting was used to the dry heat of Israel, not the cold damp of England. Even so, the plant was doing well ... until I re-potted it in British soil. It soon became apparent in order for it to survive it needed "special care."

Like my little olive branch, maybe you also need "special care" as you embark on lifting your vision higher. Perhaps in the past you have not experienced a fruitful life, or even fruitful relationships.

Today I want to encourage you, the grace of God is sufficient for your life. When you abide in Jesus, the vine of God, the fruit of blessing, healing, provision, and peace will start to sprout all around you. God is saying, "Look and see what I will do."

Just as the orchard needs the farmer's skilled care, so our lives need tending in order to achieve their potential fruitfulness. God the Father is the head Gardener, but we must take responsibility for following His instructions in our lives.

When we take ownership of our "unfruitful branches" that need to be pruned, the fruit our lives— our produce—multiplies quickly.

The parable of the sower (Mark 4) shows how the same seed yields different fruit depending on the soil it is planted in. It's so easy to settle for inferior fruit in our lives. I encourage you to cultivate every area of your life to bear prize winning fruit!

I want to help you take an honest look at different areas of your life. I ask you to read this book with openness and a willing heart, and to be sensitive to the prompting of the Holy Spirit. I encourage you to "be real" with yourself, and I nudge you with love, to prepare for a new season as we dig up the soil, add the nutrients, compost, and water needed for your growth.

Contribution by Janet Angela Mills

"God blessed them and said, 'Be fruitful and increase in number and fill the water in the seas, and let the birds increase on the earth'" (Genesis 1:22). This is the first scripture that always comes to mind when I hear the word "fruitfulness." One of the greatest manifestations of fruitfulness in our lives is the beautiful and rare treasures to heaven—our children. Joshua and I have dedicated our lives completely to walk in the divine plans and purposes that our Heavenly Father has for us and our two children, Lincoln and Liberty. We give God thanks for the revelation of His glory, goodness, and grace!

We have learned there is no other way to live than in His realms of glory—full of health, wealth, and happiness for our spirit, soul, and body. We choose to believe His Word on purpose, and to put our trust completely in His promises.

One of the greatest revelations God has taught me is the power of our words. Our words are seeds! They create after their kind. We can speak words of life which produce overwhelming blessings, or we can speak words of death which create endless despair.

"The tongue has the power of life and death, and those who love it will eat its fruit" (Proverbs 18:21). God has shown me the power of declaring His glory! As I choose to speak God's Living Word over my life, fruitfulness comes forth. As fruitfulness grows, it flourishes and multiplies! We need to have a passion and an immense love for God's Word. His Word is life to every part of our being!

"For the word of God is alive and active. Sharper than any double-edged sword, it penetrates even to dividing soul and spirit, joints and marrow; it judges the thoughts and attitudes of the heart" (Hebrews 4:12).

When I was pregnant with both of my children, I spoke God's will over my physical body and over my babies within my womb. I declared God's glory over every area and sphere of my babies' lives. I prophesied God's Word into their destinies, decreed divine health, favor, blessings, and increase. We believed for God to give them an immense sensitivity to the Holy Spirit, and that they would be led by His wisdom and revelation each day of their lives. We believed I would have a supernatural pregnancy, labor, and delivery! I can testify that both my deliveries were supernatural and full of miracles.

Today both of my children have a heart after God and His glory. Lincoln has experienced many God encounters and knows the power of prayer. He understands the principles of sowing and reaping in finances, in time, and in relationship. Liberty lives in a realm of joy and freedom. She manifests the revelation of "No Limits." We are so thankful that we can travel (most of the time) together as a family. The nations are our inheritance and we are walking His Word out together! Our children are our most favorite fruit!

Janet Angela Mills
Co-Founder of New Wine International Ministries, Inc.
Vancouver, B.C. Canada | Palm Springs, CA, USA
www.newwineinternational.org

Chapter Two

The Neglected Garden

I went by the field of the lazy man,

And by the vineyard of the man
devoid of understanding;

And there it was, all overgrown with thorns;

Its surface was covered with nettles;

Its stone wall was broken down.

When I saw it, I considered it well;

I looked on it and received instruction:

A little sleep, a little slumber,

A little folding of the hands to rest;

So shall your poverty come like a prowler,
And your need like an armed man.

Proverbs 24:30-34

When I look at photographs in magazines and see women dressed up ... with their hair looking absolutely fantastic, I wonder to myself, "How do they keep their hair so tidy and looking good?" Their hair is cut, gelled, sprayed, pinned up, and perfect.

My hair, on the other hand, seems to have a mind of its own! No matter how much money I spend on hair-cuts, products to keep hair in place, blow-drys, or clips and pins, it will only take one gust of wind to turn the beautiful creation into an absolute mess—looking much like it does when I first get up in the morning, or as I am often told, a haystack!

The same thing happens if I have done my hair and then have a fit of giggles. It seems to respond by being very fly away and wild! If you did not know me, you would think that I neglected my hair by the way it sometimes looks.

It is easy to get frustrated and not bother when all my efforts are dashed by a gust of wind, but if I didn't try and do something, I know I would be aware of the state of my hair and probably embarrassed by it. It is not vanity for vanity's sake, but just trying to make the best of what God gave me—and that happens to be wild, fly-away hair!

A Little Folding of the Hands ...

The farm where we keep our horses is set in a beautiful countryside and was known for the high equestrian standard there. The farmer and his wife ran a very professional, high-class establishment and always had a long waiting list of people interested in keeping their horses there.

The farm machinery was kept in barns throughout the winter. There were no broken fences and they kept a very smart stable yard. Their whole life had been invested in this farm, and they had great motivation as a team to be excellent in everything they did.

Six years ago the farmer's wife, who was a dear friend of mine, died after a two year battle with cancer. It was sad to walk back on the yard and find her "ever so big" presence no longer there.

Slowly things started to change. The farmer lost interest in everything. When a fence broke, it was not mended. Tractors were left out and stood in the field, rusty and broken down. Fields started to suffer through lack of care, and the stable yard had weeds growing all over it. The more broken down everything got, the more despondent he became, not seeing a way out. Though it was not deliberate neglect, in his grief he just could not be bothered, and let things go.

As time has gone on, his heart is healing and his hope for the future is being restored. With much help and encouragement, he now wants to repair anything broken, tidy up, and get the yard back to its former glory. The fields and farm look super and he is back to having a waiting list of prospective clients who would like to stable their horses there.

The Price of Neglect

There is a neglect that is deliberate and comes from the place of, "Oh, I can't be bothered. I will do it tomorrow," or, "Why should I do anything when someone else can do it." Laziness, selfishness, or a sheer lack of discipline can not only make others frustrated with you, but it can actually isolate you from people.

When you have this mind-set of neglect, things can quickly spiral down into decay and hopelessness. You will grow despondent. Soon things are so far out of hand that you can be overwhelmed by what it would take to restore order. It is easy to give up.

Lance Wallnau says, "How you do anything is how you do everything." This is true. If you cannot even be bothered to have discipline in your life, then what does that say for your walk with God? Do you have the same "I can't be bothered" mind-set with Him? If others are blessed and you are not, do you grumble? Do you get angry and look to criticize others if they point something out to you?

If that's you then it's time to grow up. Stop making excuses and do what you say you will do. Get to work on what you know needs to be done.

Above all, do not neglect your relationship with God. He is not neglecting His relationship with you. He loves you too much to do that!

Are there areas of neglect in your life? Is there evidence of neglect in your relationship with God? If so, I encourage you today to let Father God take your hand and take you higher with Him. You see, His grace is sufficient for you—He will not judge or condemn. But neither will He compromise. He will stretch you and test you in all your weak areas so that you become stronger. Don't let excuses stop you from moving forward.

It's time to break up the fallow ground!

Contibution by William Imes

As I began to think about the neglected garden, memories of my past started to surface. I was raised on a farm in Northwest Ohio—a very large garden if you will. This garden was over 500 acres, which was quite large for those days. On our garden (farm) we raised grain crops. We also had 1,000 pigs and 200 steers. This was our livelihood.

My dad was continually talking to me about "The Land" and he would say, "Son, take care of the land, and it will take care of you." A good farmer is a true husbandman and caretaker of the land, and my dad knew those 500 acres intimately. He knew the personality of each field. He would tell me, pointing to a certain area, "This field has a low area and holds water late in the spring. It will not produce much unless we get proper drainage."

Pointing to another portion he would say, "That field has a very sandy hill and will not hold moisture, so the crops will not produce if we don't plant it at the proper time."

For another patch he would tell me, "That field has a very hard clay knob and will need to be cultivated several times to break up the soil into particles small enough to get good soil/seed contact."

Each field needed to be fertilized differently, depending on the seed to be planted. For example, corn needed different ratios of fertilizer than soybeans or wheat. The quality of the soil where it would be planted must be considered as well.

As the crops grew, they still needed to be tended. My dad showed me how to make sure the plant was getting the proper nutrition for a good harvest. It was important to check on the plants while they were small for this was the time to add whatever additional fertilizer or minerals were needed. Colour was a big clue to indicate what was missing. Corn that was beginning to have a yellow look was a sign of low nitrogen, and red or purple hues were a sign of low phosphorous and would need potash to be added.

So it was during those early years, while learning to tend the fields on my father's farm, that I learned about "process" and "harvest." I observed the natural laws of our world, the God-given principles that we need to follow—whether in a garden or in my construction business which I have cultivated for more than forty years.

Buildings need to be set on solid foundations. The interior or your house needs to be protected with sturdy walls and well-maintained paint or siding. The roof needs to be in good condition to keep out the elements of rain and snow. Windows need to be caulked to keep out the wind.

It is vitally important to pay attention to the tending phase. You must not let upkeep on any of these areas go unnoticed or unattended for a period of time. If you do, major problems begin to develop. The worst is a slow water leak that works quietly behind the scenes, and by the time you finally notice it, major renovation is required.

You see people every day that are building their lives on solid foundations. They are reading their Bible, praying regularly, going to church, etc., but soon a slow leak begins to penetrate the building. Problems begin to appear with their business, finances, kids' issues at school, and the pressures of life. Unattended problems—a neglected garden—can lead to even more destruction. Just like damage from a slow water leak, walls begin to crumble and a good life can fall apart.

Observing life as a farmer and then as a builder has taught me that our lives need to be tended to like my dad's fields of corn, or my construction business building homes. It's like the parable of the Sower in the Bible. Seed cast on wet soil gets no air and suffocates. Many lives get suffocated with television, the Internet, social media, financial problems, marital issues, or work. Other lives are like the seed planted on the sandy hill—the water drains out too fast and the nutrients of life drain away with it. Gradually, this life produces very little.

You may know someone who is like the hard clay knob. When you cast seed on this soil, it just lays there and dries up, or maybe some vermin eats the seed before it has a chance to sprout. Perhaps you have a family member or friend that you have opened your heart to and cast good seed only to have them reject your advice. Don't give up on them! Continue to pray for the Lord to soften their heart. Pray for the Holy Spirit to soften the hard soil in their heart so they will receive the right nutrients, tend their garden, and produce a fruitful life.

William Imes
Business Owner
Ohio, USA

Chapter Three

The Damaged Garden

My husband, Martin, loves to make the garden look beautiful. We relish every moment when everything looks tidy, in place, and blooming. It is pure joy to look out on a well-tended garden. One big problem we have is Breeze!

Breeze is the new companion we got for our dog Daisy, after our eldest dog Poppy died. My daughter suggested we adopt a dog from the rescue centre instead of getting a new puppy, which sounded like a good idea at the time.

As we walked past all the windows of the dogs to be re-homed, our eyes caught sight of Breeze. After several visits, we decided we would adopt her. We had been told she had been starved and then dumped by her gypsy owner. They told us she needed lots of exercise, that she didn't like cats, and was prone to escaping! We felt we could cope with that, as she was so loving. We took her home.

What they didn't tell us, and we soon discovered all on our own, was that she chews anything inside or outside the house. She digs holes everywhere, kicks up the grass, and likes to trample all over the flower beds, digging up the bulbs and roots of plants! She also likes to eat flowers, steal the fruit from the trees, and sit in the large basket our olive tree is planted in, perched on top of all the crocuses and snowdrops surveying her land! If you saw our garden right now, it would look more like a rugby field than a garden. It's quite funny really because she is so naughty, but does it with such joy!

Breeze has damaged our garden, but in time we will put it right, smarten things up, and hopefully she will choose not to continue this destructive behaviour!

Hidden Damage

A damaged garden is easy to spot. Overturned plants and exposed bulbs can be seen by even the most casual observer, but when lives are damaged, it may not be so obvious.

Some years ago we were part of a church just outside London. One Sunday morning a new family came to visit the church and decided they would like to attend on a regular basis.

From the first meeting with them, with their two small boys and baby girl, we knew this was a dysfunctional family. The boys behaved badly, and the parents seemed to have no control over them. Many of the other children in church were frightened of them. If they saw a scrap of food fall on the floor, they would immediately dive to eat it—that was my first warning sign. As a mother myself, I noticed the little girl was always strapped in the pram. I can't remember her being held by them, and when she had her bottle of milk it was attached to the side of the pram and her head positioned so it would stay in her mouth.

I was overseeing the Sunday school at that time and my warning antennas went straight up. A friend and I arranged a "pastoral visit" to get to know a little more about this family in their home.

The first time, they knew we were coming. Although the house was smelly and absolutely filthy, and the TV was kept on so loudly it was hard to talk, we still had an open conversation about their backgrounds. Both had been abused as children, and the husband had been in a mental health hospital for a brief spell. The wife, who was obviously uncomfortable talking to us, told us how much she loved her children and wanted to protect them as she was not protected when she was younger. They told us the boys were at a playgroup and the baby was sleeping. We prayed with them both and then had a time of ministry to the wife. Despite our time together, I had a nagging feeling that something was wrong. I felt that we should immediately bring in a child care specialist to help them both, but the person with me advised me to "take it to prayer" and that no other action was required. In my naivety I listened to her despite my concerns.

As we were leaving, we had to walk through the kitchen to go out and I saw the husband pushing twelve tiny kittens from their cat into a very small box, one on top of the other. The poor things were squealing and crying out, and then to my absolute horror, he started to tape the box up tightly. Being an animal lover, I instinctively grabbed the box from him, trying to rip it open to let the kittens breathe. He just laughed and found it very funny. He told us that he didn't want them and planned to drown them in the river behind the house, and I could see he meant it. He had put a rock in the bottom of the box.

I left the house, box in hand, with twelve small kittens. As soon as I got to my car and managed to open the box, I cried at what I had just seen. I took them to a friend who runs a rescue centre who cared for them. My concern for the family heightened. If someone could do this to an animal, what might they do to a child? Why did we not see the children?

My spirit was disturbed that night. The Holy Spirit prompted me to insist that we go back again. We returned unannounced to the house the next day. Our plan was to help start to clean up for them and to double check things. Thank goodness I listened to that prompt.

The Damaged Garden

When the couple opened the door we were met with shocked, embarrassed faces, but they did let us in. We couldn't see the children anywhere, but this time with the television off, I heard soft crying upstairs. They were reluctant for me to go upstairs, but I just knew the children were up there. I found the bedroom doors tied to the banister so that they could not be opened from the inside. In one room I found the two little boys (five-years-old and three-years-old) tied to their beds and there were bars on the windows where they had obviously tried to escape before. There were no linens or blankets of any kind. Excrement was all over the walls and urine soaked through their clothes and mattress. What was so upsetting to me was how frightened they seemed, afraid I would hurt them if they made a sound.

The little baby girl was locked in the other room by herself. The room was dark and she was silent. She didn't make a sound even when she heard my voice. When I removed the cover on her pram, she was not only tightly strapped in with a baby harness, the smell of rancid milk all over her hit me. Her pram bed was soaked and dirty, she had severely bleeding skin on her bottom as she had no "nappy" (diaper) and had been lying in her poo. Her skin was inflamed and sore. This beautiful little girl was only six months old. It looked like she may have had a sight problem as she didn't seem to focus properly. I felt the tears of Jesus as I held her. It was all I could do not to throw up with the smell.

All three children were placed into care that day. Because of government laws, we were not able to look after them or foster as I had been willing to do. It was heart breaking. We have held these three children up to God in prayer asking Father God to heal the experiences they went through so that the repeat cycle stops here.

The parents disappeared from the house the next day never to be seen again.

The reason I am sharing this is because as I have pondered, prayed, and talked through this many times, I have realised that this couples' experiences had so traumatized them, that as much as they wanted to have children, they simply had no other experience to compare to. They had no frame of reference, and therefore, probably repeated just what had been done to them.

Damage Can Be Repaired

Perhaps abuse or neglect has not been your experience. Maybe you have been scarred by an accident or bereavement. Maybe you have suffered rape, walked through a painful divorce, or suffered a broken heart.

I want to tell you there is hope. Your past does not define your future. God specializes in restoring damaged gardens to fruitfulness!

You need not justify the way things are in light of how things have been. You can begin today. You have the power of choice. You can stop the damage and say, "No more!" You can choose how you will respond to negative words, thoughts, or deeds. Come into agreement with God's plan to repair and restore this very moment! Nothing is greater than His power. No amount of damage compares to His ability to make all things new. Connect to Him and allow Him to replant what has been uprooted or distressed.

He alone can bring beautiful, perfect produce from injured plants. He can return your garden back to the original design with no trace of the "damager" present. When submitted to God, your pain becomes fertilizer. Watered by the Word and breathed on by the Spirit, life comes again—vibrant, healthy, and whole.

Contribution by Lance Wallnau

We live in a world that Jesus described as increasingly lawless and without self control. This breeds a culture of victimization and entitlement. When you hear, "This always happens to me," or "You won't believe what they just did to me," it is evidence that the last days are upon us. At its core, this is a denial of our personal power to create our own experience. Think of the world as Jesus described it—a field "that brings forth of itself."

"The field is the world," He said. A field does not argue with a farmer, it simply produces whatever is sown into it. Likewise, the world around us. It is a reflection of our interior life.

Even the "unfair" and "unjust" harvests of life are to a degree, our own creations. Our circumstances may not always be ours in creation, but they become ours by the way we respond to them. What if "the field" doesn't just respond to us—what if it IS us? What if every time you expend energy to explain, justify, or defend yourself, you are giving up a portion of your personal power to create the life you truly want? Or put another way, if you only own 90% of your thoughts, feelings, and behaviors, you've given the devil a 10% foothold in your life!

That's not to say that any of us are so powerful that we can independently reshape our lives apart from the ability that God gives us. Like Kim teaches, when the garden is damaged it takes time to detect and arrest deterioration and cultivate health. The point is nothing starts until you exercise the power of commitment, and commitment can't happen if you deny your own power of choice. The sail on a great ship does not move the ship, it simply catches the wind. We make a choice to stop being victims, and in that moment we reset the sail to catch winds of grace to move us in a new direction.

Years ago, Steven Covey introduced the concept that "responsibility" is "response-ability" it's the ability to respond. You have that fraction of a second of awareness before any voluntary action is taken. In that fraction you can exercise "response-ability." But think about this; the body has a unique ability to create receptors to feelings that produce pleasure or pain, and any experience repeated often enough will actually cause a sort of addiction to that feeling. Every experience you have forms a pattern. Feelings that fire together wire together, and this is something even the enemy knows. There is an element of spiritual warfare in every garden. The enemy seeks to create experiences that form beliefs and lock in feelings that lead to decisions that produce harvests.

This is the story of entire nations who have a history of warfare or pain that leads to deep roots of prejudice and distrust, the fruit of which we see in wars and acts of terrorism. This is all because thoughts and feelings not judged and brought captive to God's truth will fester into bondage.

Be very certain, spirits seek to forge unhealthy chemical cravings in the brain and body. There are approximately 100 billion neurons in the brain and each one has 1,000 to 10,000 synapses, or places where they can connect with other neurons. Imagine that every neuron represents a thought, memory, or unit of information. As these networks mesh, complex ideas, memories, and emotions form. Certain cells carry receptors that dock with chemicals of pleasure and pain. Once the docking takes place, a pattern can potentially form. The body will seek the chemical experience. This is the story behind all addictions.

Humans form these receptors quite easily for good or ill.

Can you see why the anointing is such a powerful thing? The Word of God and the anointing can sweep through this part of your garden and take away destructive influence and make a place for new ideas, memories, and healthy desires. Chemicals, feelings, thoughts, spirits, neuro-networks ... it is all real and all subject to the power of the blood of Jesus, the Word, and the anointing. You can be transformed by the renewing of your mind, and as you can see, there is a whole lot more going on in this transformation process than we thought.

I've seen people set free in a moment of time and watched their physical facial features change—like a miracle makeover that made women ten years younger in appearance. Some of these transformations have been recorded on video in my own meetings. The truth does set us free, but it never frees us in territory we classify as "victim" or "bitter" or "unforgiven." There is a mystery in all this, but somehow it makes sense.

I went to Kim Corden's prayer cottage in the UK and felt the restorative power of the Spirit. You can actually create sacred space where you live and invite God to inhabit it. She understands the inward and outward journey of unconditional love and the power of God's Spirit to transform the soul. Like any good gardener, you have to get down into the dirt and on your knees, but the soul of man is made for dominion in the garden. It is where we were originally formed.

No matter what level of damage your garden has experienced, you can begin to set it to rights this moment. It begins with a choice. Decide now to allow the Holy Spirit unfettered access to restore all.

Dr. Lance Wallnau
President, The Lance Learning Group
www.lancelearning.com
Fort Worth, Texas, USA

Tending Your Garden

Part Two

The Areas in Your Garden

Tending Your Garden

Chapter Four

Tending Your Secret Garden

The secret garden is my favourite garden, where I love to dwell.

I live in England and there are many old mansions with huge gardens. Some of them have a "secret garden," usually equipped with a gate in order to enter. It is always a place of quiet tranquility. Most often there is a fountain or the sound of quietly running water. The fragrance of roses and summer flowers fills the air, along with lots of little birds tweeting and singing. Artists love to be in the secret garden as they get so much inspiration from the atmosphere. Sitting and reading a book in such a place brings every word on the page alive.

Delightful as this is, my secret garden is very different.

My secret garden is a place in the spirit where my Jesus and I dwell together, spend time together, and just "be." It is a place to meet with my "Bridegroom," and a place I never want to leave. It is deep within my very being and no-one else can go there—just as you have your own secret garden, meant for you and God alone.

I used to think that I walked in and out of the secret garden, until I came to the realisation that I can dwell there all the time, wherever I am. I never have to leave!

It is personal and intimate. It is filled with pure love.

I don't really notice the garden. The garden is just the backdrop, the atmosphere. It is the One who is IN the garden that I am focused on.

When you discover this place—when you experience the depth of love Jesus has for you, the total acceptance, and the oneness with Him—it is painful to be away.

In the secret garden you will meet with the Trinity: Father, Son, and Holy Spirit as William P. Young describes so beautifully in his book *The Shack*.

How do I get there? How do I enter that place? For me it can be in a breath, but always when I enter into worship, I am ushered right there. I am sure you have your personal way to connect with God in this place..

When I am there time stands still. In the beautiful quiet, in the "being" together, Father God whispers the most outrageous assignments to me. He asks me to step out into unknown situations, and all I can say is YES to Him. Unafraid. Totally secure.

It is only when I step back into what people call reality that I realise what I have agreed to! It seems so easy when I am standing in the secret place breathing the breath of God. Then when I must encounter people and practicality, I think to myself, "Oh my, now I have to walk it out!"

Have you ever been in this place? Have you discovered your secret garden with Jesus?

If you haven't, but have always desired to have this intimate relationship with God, I encourage you to sit down and look at your life, your experiences and thoughts, and ask God to help you understand the block stopping you.

It might be fear of having a personal encounter with God because you feel unworthy. It could be because of experiences in the past where you have trusted someone, but they have betrayed your trust. It could be that you have yet to discover it is not about how you feel about yourself, but how He feels about you!

If you believe the Bible is the true Word of God, you will know time and time again it talks about the love of God and how God looks at our heart, not our sin.

You have not been forgotten, and nothing you have done can separate you from God except your choice to be separated. I find that praying in tongues is a most excellent way to develop the secret garden of your spirit (Jude 20).

Without a personal encounter with God, it is hard to have stability. Get familiar with your "gate" to the secret garden so you can dwell there. Know what it takes for you to enter a quiet place where nothing exists between you and God. Learn to live in the secret garden.

In the earth, we are running out of time. We feel the urgency. In the heavenly place there is no rush, no pressure, but there is a purpose God has for you in that place. The first purpose is to receive His love, to be restored and renewed. As much as you love Him and want to give your adoration to Him, you will never, never outdo His love for you!

Let me ask you: what are you passionate for? Your car? The things you like to do? Your holidays, your secret desires? Or is it first and foremost, intimacy with Jesus—in His garden of love?

You may fool men with an outward appearance, but you cannot fool God.

Dare to believe you can walk straight into a secret garden with Father God. Your life will be marked by it. You will be wrecked by it, and having experienced it yourself, you can help others find the "hidden gate" to their secret garden.

I invite you to read *The Chronicles of Narnia* by C.S. Lewis. The lamppost will show you the way!

Contribution by Wendy K. Walters

The pace of life has grown very busy. We shuffle from place to place, tending to responsibilities and keeping track of our families, finances, and friends. We long for significance as we scurry about meeting needs—dreaming of a day when we can slow down and enjoy life.

Learning to dwell in the secret place (my secret garden), reverencing the presence of God, and spending time in worship and in prayer has been my antidote. I am called on daily to exercise high levels of creativity and resourcefulness. I am a mover and a shaker with high productivity. People depend on me to touch heaven, respond to the whisper of God, and emerge with practical, actionable solutions. I can only do this when I make His heart my habitation.

As a small girl, I experienced the tangible presence of God, and it has been real to me ever since. There is nothing I love so much as singing and worshipping, and bringing heaven to earth! I love it so much, that it is as much a part of me as breathing or eating.

I spent many years as a worship pastor, and I am now privileged to travel and speak, consult for platform and product development, coach authors and help them publish their books. The funny thing is, I still dwell in the secret garden—even more so than when my paid profession was worship! I set the atmosphere in my office. When I speak, I bring heaven's atmosphere into the room before I utter a word (even at completely secular business conferences). My sphere of influence expands when I bring heaven to bear. Just like when King Saul was comforted and calmed as David played the harp in his presence.

When times got rough for us and our business—and things got very bleak indeed—knowing how to dwell in the secret garden saved me. It was vital for me to regularly experience and fellowship God's reality in spite of the extreme contradiction of my circumstances.

Like Kim, I don't come and go out of the secret garden—I live there. At times I am keenly aware, and at other times it is much more in the background. But it is only here, when I am tuned in to His voice, that He gives me the outrageous creativity I need to help my clients. It is when I am in communion with the Spirit of God that my best ideas (the most profitable ones) come into being. When I am in unity with the Spirit, I am unstoppable—and you are too.

I was mentored by someone who taught me to "practice the presence of God." He literally meant that I was to pull away by myself, sit in front of my piano, close my eyes, and sing a new song to the Lord. He encouraged me to stay there in that place until my voice was in tune with God's and I had entered into the rhythm of heaven. It was in this atmosphere that I learned to prophesy. It was in these moments that God showed me pictures of my outrageous future and

I believed they were possible because the power of God was so palpable when He showed them to me.

I adore spending time with God's people and love the synergy of the corporate setting, but that isn't enough. An uncommon life requires uncommon choices. The choice to steal away with Jesus and turn down the noise in my life long enough to focus on His joy is a consistent source of hope, comfort, and success.

If you have never done this, it may feel strange at first. Like anything new or uncharted, it is often unnatural in the beginning. You might feel awkward, or that you aren't doing something right if you aren't having some amazing vision or audible-voice-of-God moment. Give yourself some grace. Set your affection toward the Lord and you will soon find that you cannot live without this time alone with Him.

Here are some suggestions to cultivate the atmosphere of heaven and learn to dwell in your very own secret garden.

1. **Get alone.** I don't care if it is in your car, your closet, or your bathroom—just get away all by yourself!

2. **Get quiet.** Turn down the ambient noise around you. Turn the cell phone off. Don't check email. No television or background "conflicters." Find a peaceful place where you will not be distracted, even if it can be only for a few minutes.

3. **Set the atmosphere.** I like to change things up. Some days I begin with high energy praise music. Other times I like having quiet meditation music or sounds of nature. Sometimes I want absolute stillness—especially if I can be near a fireplace, a fountain, or the ocean. I will set the lighting, I may even light candles or fill the room with a fragrance ... whatever brings me joy and causes me to want to linger in that place.

4. **Invite God.** Just that simply, I ask God to come and join me. I let Him know I have stolen away and would love to spend some time with Him ... He never disappoints! He has always been available to meet with me, every single time!

5. **Start with gratitude.** There is a hymn that goes: "Count your blessings, name them one by one, count your many blessings see what God has done." Extol His virtue and lift up His accomplishments. Take note of all He has orchestrated in your life and how many good things are a result of God's favor and blessing.

6. **Linger as long as you can.** The more time you spend with Him, the more you will become like Him and step into who you were created to be!

Wendy K. Walters
Consultant, Director of Publications
www.wendykwalters.com | www.palmtreeproductions.com
Fort Worth, Texas, USA

Chapter Five

Tending Your Soul

Those who really know me would say I am a person who lives "in the moment." Memories are precious to me, but there is nothing like the excitement of the "now."

We all love to tell stories and reminisce about good, happy times. When we do, our heart feels glad. When we talk about difficult or sad times, we sometimes re-live the anguish and pain—it is like it all comes flooding back again and our heart fills with emotion.

As a person who lives in the moment, I also "feel" the moment. One area that always brings a twinge to my heart is the loss of our babies.

Martin and I have four children—precious children, three sons and a daughter. We would have had nine children if all had gone well, but it did not.

While on our honeymoon in Rhodes, Greece during May 1981, I became pregnant with our first baby. I did not even know I was pregnant until the day the excruciating pains of miscarriage started. I remember the doctor coming to examine me and saying I had lost the baby, "but it was no major disaster." To us, it was. Although Martin and I were surrounded by love, the sadness of the day marked our hearts. We gave our little one to God, but did not know we would have to lift other babies we would never see to heaven. One baby died in the womb. I saw it moving on the scan the week before, but then, more sadness. Because it was a late pregnancy and I had not miscarried, the infant had to be surgically removed. I prayed for this little life to be resurrected, but God called it home. I was a young Christian at the time, but even during those distressing times, my faith never doubted that God is good, even though I did not understand why this was happening.

In between we had our beautiful babies, and each one is unique and special. The last miscarriage I experienced was the worst for me. Grief hit me because God had clearly given me the baby's name, and I knew her in the spirit.

I dream a lot and live my dreams. My spirit is always awake! One night I woke up and I heard young children laughing. They were happy and they were waving at me.

I saw a cloud, but in the cloud was a green garden. There were many flowers and I remember a swing hanging from a tree. There they were, our little ones. I could not fully see their faces as they were blurred but I heard them laughing and my spirit knew they were loved and happy. I knew I would see them face to face the day I enter heaven. Why did Father God give me a glimpse of them? It was to heal my heart because without healed emotions, I could not be of full use to Him.

Become Aware

Take a moment to place your hands on either side of your head. Pause and listen. What do you hear? Peaceful silence, or conversation and chatter? How do you feel? How is your posture and breathing? How aware are you of the multitude of thoughts that run through your mind in a twenty-four hour period?

At times there seems to be so much noise and disruption inside our minds, especially when we try to quiet our thoughts. As we become aware of our thoughts and feelings, we can choose what we welcome and what needs to be rejected. I have had to train my mind to be quiet when I tell it to, and take control over my thought life. Otherwise the thoughts would take control over me!

I particularly want you to become aware of the negative conversations where we "talk to ourselves," so you can stop them and bring your mind back into line with the truth of the Bible to have the mind of Christ. You must learn to "... take the helmet of salvation, and the sword of the Spirit which is the Word of God" (Ephesians 6: 17).

The images we see in day-to-day life, in movies and on the television, really do go deep into our subconscious. Even after we have turned them off, these things "play on" in our minds, especially if they have been disturbing images. We can have nightmares or panic attacks from what we have seen, or we can sleep peacefully having the most beautiful dreams after seeing pleasant, happy images.

Have a Healthy Mind

Bitterness and hate are two emotions that can cause so much harm. Once they take hold in your mind, they can be difficult to control. Everything you see around you will be affected by your thoughts and then often, be demonstrated by your actions.

Thank goodness for forgiveness. When we come to the foot of the Cross and ask for forgiveness, it is done. We no longer have to allow these feelings and thoughts to even be part of our thinking.

We can walk in freedom having a healthy mind, godly thoughts, and being in full control of what goes on in our minds. Most importantly, we have the choice to dwell on the right thoughts and nothing else! "Whatever is true, whatever is honourable, whatever is right, whatever is pure, whatever is lovely, whatever is of good repute, if there is any excellence and if there is anything worthy of praise, dwell on these things" (Philippians 4:8).

Your soul is one of the most important areas to tend. So take a good look. Picture your soul, your emotions, your mind and your will in God's hands. Be honest with yourself, what do you see?

To quote the romantic poet William Wordsworth:

"Your mind is the garden,

your thoughts are the seeds,

the harvest can either be flowers or weeds."

If we are to pray without hindrances, free from our own motives, we need a clean, pure, beautifully healthy heart (inner being). I believe it is possible for our souls to be fully alive, perfectly healthy, and tuned to the heart of God every single second of every single day of our lives. That is true freedom: to live, breathe, and have your heart beat in rhythm with God's heart.

Oh, what a powerful place to pray from!

Contribution by Nick Try

As Lance Wallnau addressed delegates at one of his Cabo San Lucas Dream trips, I experienced a "paradigm shift." To realise that we could take the initiative to manage our emotional state through changing our body position or focus in order to raise our performance was so liberating!

As I read scripture, particularly the Psalms, I see believers such as King David taking that responsibility as he confronts his soul about why it is in despair (Psalm 42:6 and 43:5) and then refocuses it on the goodness of God, or tells his soul to bless the Lord with all that is within him (Psalm 103).

We can see the consequences for a believer who failed to manage their soul. This was the case for Elijah, having seen God send fire from heaven as he humiliated the 450 prophets of Baal (1 Kings 18), then ran away and hid in a cave to have a pity party after receiving a death threat from Jezebel (1 Kings 19).

For twenty years I worked for UK Defence Contractor GEC-Marconi. Following its acquisition by British Aerospace to form BAE SYSTEMS, I decided to apply for voluntary severance to develop the intercessory work Kim and I had been doing with Beacon Ministries. As my leaving date approached and I had to decide what to do with various records and documents, I became aware that my soul was grieving. The Lord showed me how my sense of identity was linked to projects that I had undertaken, and that it was time to release them to define my identity in who I am in Christ Jesus. It quickly brought a powerful release.

A season of working with the Holy Spirit as He leads us to reappraise the significance of the meaning of events in our lives is typically an indicator that God has an "upgrade" planned for us, but that old thought patterns are not compatible with the things ahead. In this case, the things weren't bad, but I had unwittingly attached the wrong meaning to them.

The same principle applies to "bad" events too. If you find an area of your life blocked or "disempowered" by what happened, then I have news for you: Your future is not defined by your past, but by the promises of God. God has release and renewal for your soul if you will release the meaning that you are applying to these events and let Him show you how He will redeem the situation through his empowering grace.

In fact, just last October God ambushed me as Randy Bixby was speaking on this subject in Dallas! I was oblivious to the depth and power of emotion associated with a particular event, but as I was talking to Randy afterwards the Holy Spirit spoke to me from 2 Corinthians 1:3-4:

"Blessed be the God and Father of our Lord Jesus Christ, the Father of mercies and God of all comfort, who comforts us in all our affliction so that we will be able to comfort those who are in any affliction with the comfort we ourselves are comforted by God."

Though I may never fully understand why things happened the way they did, I know that He does, and that as I walk in His comfort I am empowered to bring breakthrough for others. As Jesus put it, "Heal the sick, raise the dead, cleanse the lepers, cast out demons. Freely you have received, freely give" (Mathew 10:8).

Tending Your Garden

God has equipped you with the gifts to fulfill your calling. You have the power to fulfill your potential through tending your soul, or to sabotage it through neglecting it.

Let's end this chapter with something practical that you can apply. Speak these words of David from Psalm 103 out loud to your soul. It's time to tell it that things are going to be different around here from now on!

Bless the Lord, O my soul,

And all that is within me, bless His holy name.

Bless the Lord, O my soul,

And forget none of His benefits;

Who pardons all your iniquities,

Who heals all your diseases;

Who redeems your life from the pit,

Who crowns you with lovingkindness
and compassion;

Who satisfies your years with good things,

So that your youth is renewed like the eagle.

Nick Try
Partner, Try Solutions
Director of Integritytech Ltd.
UK

Chapter Six

Tending Your Body

I have just joined a local health club that offers every form of exercise you could need; gym programmes, cycling, aerobics, Pilates, boxing, swimming, and the latest dance craze classes. It also offers the much more appealing jacuzzi, steam, sauna, and beauty treatments!

I went for a review with a gym trainer and was given a programme that seemed very difficult to start with, but "No pain, no gain!" So I agreed. (Determination will definitely be needed to keep this up!)

Walking back to the changing room after a really hard gym session I saw a poster that read: "Inch Loss Wrap—Immediate Results."

"Hmmm," I thought, "is there an easier way to trim up?" After all, that was just what the poster offered.

I went to inquire and an extremely persuasive therapist suggested I book a six-week course, as there was a special offer on. Before I knew it, I had agreed. I had never done anything like this before but thought I would give it a go.

The Process

- **Step One:** They give you disposable underwear to put on and then scrub your skin with a brush to exfoliate and open the pores. (Ouch!) Then comes the embarrassing part (girls, you know what I mean) of measuring you all over.

- **Step Two:** You are covered from neck to toe in a thick grey mud that smells of Fennel.

- **Step Three:** Hot bandages are then wrapped around you tightly so you end up looking like an Egyptian mummy. You waddle to the nearby table and the attendant somehow gets you up onto it!

- **Step Four:** You are wrapped in shrink wrap and lie on a bed covered in an aluminium foil blanket.

- **Step Five:** Cook for one hour!

- **Step Six:** Unwrap all the bandages and then get remeasured and, guess what, to my absolute surprise I lost an accumulative eleven inches in one treatment!

- **Step Seven:** Now the talk. I didn't know there was one! This was an explanation of the whole process.

I can just hear you thinking to yourself, "Does it really work? Where can I have it done, and how much does it cost?" Hang on though, there is a snag.

Firstly, yes, it really does work!

How? The clay and bandages are full of minerals that detoxify your body and continue working over a period of time.

How long does it last? Ahhhhhhh ... now you are asking the right question, and the one question I forgot to ask when I signed up for the treatment! The inch loss treatment is really a kick start to your body to detox, and it will only last as long as you continue to feed your body the right foods, drink enormous amounts of water to flush out the toxins, and exercise regularly, AND ... wait for it ... if you don't, then you can continue the treatments, which means more cost, etc.

While I was lying on the bed talking to Father God about what I was experiencing, and how I wanted to encourage others, He said to me, "Tell them I am not a 'quick fix.' I am permanent structure in their lives!" Wow, that's powerful!

You see we can have all these treatments or go to the gym to keep our body healthy, and God loves that we do make an effort. However, what He is really after is our heart. It is good to stay in shape and look after our healthy bodies, but to be honest, it does no good at all in the long run if we have a spiritually unhealthy heart. It will eventually make us sick.

Being God's ambassador needs not only a healthy relationship with Father God, but a healthy body to be able to fulfill what He asks you to do.

When you think of your heart, how vital it is to keep you alive and how the condition of your heart physically can change the quality of life you have, you want to do everything you can to keep your heart healthy. It is so easy to take the beating of our hearts lightly, and to ignore the warning signs of illness, stress, and fatigue until it is too late and it simply stops. It is your responsibility to be a good steward of your heart.

I have found that when I am eating well, taking exercise, and getting a good night's sleep, I am more alert and have more energy. If I don't, it affects how I feel. I feel more sluggish, am prone to being distracted, and usually eat more chocolates as I haven't eaten a proper meal.

All three go together and I have learned to listen to my body and give it what it needs. When I travel this lifestyle can easily be disturbed. Jet lag really messes up your sleep patterns and airplane food does nothing for a healthy stomach!

I have now found a way to continue in what I know helps me stay healthy, rested, and focused no matter where I am and what time zone I am in. It is taking responsibility for the body God gave me.

It takes a lot of discipline and determination to stay in the routine of tending your body. Hopefully I am on the road to telling my body what to do, rather than it telling me. I need to be healthy and have the energy to be able to do what God is calling me to do. I would also be a poor witness when I talk to people about being a good steward of everything God has given us if I don't do it myself.

1 Corinthians 6:19 says, "Or do you not know that your body is a temple of the Holy Spirit who is in you, whom you have from God, and that you are not your own?"

If you take the time to think about your lifestyle, your eating habits, and your sleep patterns you may find some areas that need attention. If you have a great lifestyle then go and be a blessing to those you know need encouragement. A word spoken in love can transform someone's life.

I want to live long enough to fulfill the destiny God has given me, and I have to play my part in the preparation for that. More than that I want to be sharp spiritually—with nothing in the way of me standing in the gap on behalf of others, and have a constant communion with heaven (like a conduit) with my heart in sync with God's heart. I am prepared no matter how hard it is to pursue this place.

I want to encourage you today (and no you don't have to go and get shrink wrapped) to start from the inside out. Start from the heart and let Father God guide you to wholeness in spirit. The outer body—well, that's up to you!

Contribution by Gail Aiken

*For no one ever hated his own flesh, but nourishes
and cherishes it, just as the Lord does the church."
Ephesians 5:29*

I think that most of us would agree that it was God's design for mums and dads to nourish and cherish their child's life and that our bodies are the temple of the Holy Spirit.[1] And yet, in 2010 the World Health Organisation (WHO) estimated globally that there were 42 million children under the age of 5 who were overweight or obese, and that 81% of them live in developing countries with the trend expecting to pick up speed in developing regions over the next 10 years.[2] At the other end of the spectrum, the WHO states that we are on the brink of a demographic milestone wherein it is estimated that by 2016 the number of people over the age of 65 will outnumber children under the age of 5.[3]

On the 31st of December, 1981, while studying and working with Youth With A Mission (YWAM), I was captivated by a sunset at the Old Airport Beach in Kailua-Kona, Hawaii. A "movie" that conveyed a sense of community, but not quite like I had ever seen before, played across the skies. The breadth of the ages, abilities, and nationalities necessitated a hard look to see what they were doing. The sense of unity was quite incomprehensible. It had much to do with opportunity, pathways, the environment, but what stood out was the people who were facilitating all the activities, sport, and happenings. I was struck by who they were, their passion, their expertise, their respect, how they went about connecting with everyone—the very life in them released life into all the others. They were a team who respectfully could not do without one another, hence their divine unity corporately conveyed inspiration and a presence that oozed anointing from above. At the time, I did not understand what this picture was and I thought if I dared tell anyone what I had seen, they just might lock me in a room and throw the key away!

YWAM left an indelible imprint upon me as it demonstrated how to contribute to and realise vision from God. Some of these wonderful people encouraged me to delight in my latent athletic potential and it opened doors of connection and friendship as I competed in various tennis events, and delivered tennis coaching to some of the local Hawaiians. As I prepared to return home in 1983, I dared to share what the Lord had shown me on the 31st of December, 1981 with Dr. Bruce Thompson (Dean of College of Counselling & Health Care). I will never forget his encouragement: "despise not the day of small beginnings" and believe that "He who has begun a good work in you will bring it to completion."

The following eleven years were filled with various exploits such as pioneering new ground in setting up the first extension campus for the University of the Nations and establishing the College of Counselling & Health Care in my homeland, Australia; working at the Australian National University Canberra in the human resource area, and then with Corrective Services designing and delivering rehabilitative programs for offenders. Little did I appreciate that all of these opportunities and growing expertise were in preparation for the wildest ride of my life which some might call the journey toward convergence.

At the beginning of 1995 I took this vision of pictures and raw understandings to consultants at the Australian Sports Commission (ASC) to gauge their response. I found myself conveying a time in global history where our progress in technology and consequent demands upon family life would be such that we would see generations of children emerge that would have such significant burdens of disease that some would end up dying before their parents. At the other end of the spectrum, we would see a rapidly increasing mature aged population that might be living longer but not living stronger. Both bringing such a burden to government health systems that economies would not be able to withstand the strain.

Their response was so affirming that it marked the beginning of fifteen years research, scattered with overseas trips, to look at how governments were dealing with what was to come. The Lord was confirming what He wanted me to do, so upon returning to Australia, I began to search out and gather a group of remarkable individuals to aid me in designing and formulating programmes for the early learning years and mature aged which also included considerations for people with all forms of disability.

As I began to understand the marvels of how the brain develops and the critical milestones for maximising the wiring of the brain, I began to see how simple it is for a whole generation to end up physically inept and consequently lacking in numerous other life skills that are so necessary to fulfilling our potential. Understanding the needs in our mature years, I began to see the opportunity to meet the needs of the two generations that were on a collision course.

The solution for changing the future hope of our pre-school generations and enhancing quality of life for the SUPERgrands, to whom the responsibility has fallen for raising the children's children, lay in programmes that understood the sequencing of activities to enable the acquisition of fundamental and perceptual movement skills, but critically for the younger to make it a habit of life, the research showed that it must be done with a significant other.

After several years of research, design, and testing of programmes I took a decision to subject our programme design to scrutiny by the best of the best in our country. I was referred to Associate Professor Jeff Walkley from the Royal Melbourne Institute of Technology, Medical Sciences Department. To my delight, he agreed to spend several months pulling our program apart, interviewing, observing, using accelerometers and engaging students to collect data to arrive at a place of where he provided written academic validation to our findings. In the past several months he has honoured our business with doing the same for further programmes that we have designed and has just advised his consent to provide additional academic validation to these programs also as we prepare for international lift off.

I still find it remarkable that the essence of what the Lord imparted in 1981 was the solution to this 21st century problem!

Will you join His global health challenge? Will you apply His instructions to "nourish and cherish your flesh"? Will you, AS ONE, reclaim what the enemy is stealing from our children so that we are all expressing "Christ in us, the hope of Glory," ready for Him to "take us as His inheritance"?

Endnotes

1. 1 Corinthians 6:19-20 (KJV).

2. WebMD Health News, *Obesity in Kids Rises Around the World,* by Bill Hendrick, October 21 2010.

3. World Health Organization Global Health and Aging NIH Publication no. 11-7737, October 2011.

Gail Aiken
Managing Director, Mpowerdome
www.mpowerdome.com.au
Australia

Chapter Seven

Tending Your Relationships

I have read so many books on relationships! I have studied "How To" books on marriage, on bringing up children, and learning to work with difficult people. I have also invested in working with animals—primarily dogs and horses—in my quest to understand, get along with people, and build life-long relationships.

When I enter into any kind of relationship, it is never to get, but only to give, always believing that the relationship is for the long term. Many times my heart goes before my head! I am sure reading all these books gave me some insight and wisdom, but none of them said the same things! All had different ways of viewing relationships as each one was writing from their experiences, exploring the difficulties they had encountered, and their desire to prevent others from going through the same thing.

Let's be honest. Relationships can be absolutely wonderful, very difficult, and everything in-between! To claim that there is a perfect relationship would be hard to prove. 1 Peter 4:8 says, "Love covers a multitude of sins." It really does. Without selfless love we can never experience the relationships that God intended for us to have with one another.

Having experienced two very painful church splits over thirty years in ministry, I know first hand how someone you love and care for can suddenly turn their back on you for the sake of a title or a difference of opinion, throwing away all the trust you had in the name of the church (and God).

Maybe you have gone through something similar and have never really recovered. Maybe you find it hard to trust and build friendships at a deep level. Maybe you have been disappointed time and again—expectations unmet with the "happily ever after" part never quite manifesting.

As an emotional person, it hits my heart. Although I always forgive, I know it has made me more cautious about building new relationships. Over the last three years all of that has changed. I usually stand back now as more of an observer until I feel safe.

My healing came through working with horses. Father God used a horse, a big horse, to confront my fears.

Martin, Charlotte (my daughter), and I took two friends to see a Monty Roberts Natural Horsemanship demonstration. Monty is an American cowboy who, as a child, was treated aggressively by his horse wrangler father. The abuse did not stop with him. He saw many distressed animals marred by their experiences with his father. These animals were beaten and tied to the ground, his father believing that as he "broke their spirits" he could control them.

Monty discovered he had an affinity with horses. He realised that kindness and gentleness were the key, coupled with an authority that gave the horse confidence since they knew he was their leader.

As we sat outside the arena, we witnessed damaged, broken, and vicious horses—whose owners were scared of them, unable to control them, let alone ride them— brought in one by one.

No matter how unruly, within ten minutes we saw a frightened animal, who Monty had never met before, submit to being touched, led, and ridden. They would follow this elderly man around the arena as if in love for the first time. Many people cried at what they were witnessing. It was something very beautiful—the horse's broken spirit was restored by acts of kindness.

The icing on the cake was when Monty brought the owner of the horse into the arena. It was powerful to see the bond that was taking place, to witness the first "touch" of trust between them.

Little did I know that the following year I would be doing the same thing with Darcy, my Friesian horse. Much loved by his previous owner, he was not the one who needed the healing, I did. Now when I free lunge this beautiful animal, he so willingly and joyfully dances around the ring, and then follows me because he wants to be with me! I have a powerful time praying into relationships: for healing, for restoration, and for those abused, abandoned. While riding Darcy, I pray for those struggling to have the opportunity to discover the one and only relationship where, no matter how much you love and trust, you can never, never outdo Him, and that is with our Lord Jesus.

He will never hurt you, treat you unkindly, or abandon you—even if you abandon Him.

Before we even turn to Father, His arms are open wide for us to simply walk into. His embrace is one that you never want to be free from. There is a safety and a pure love that gives and gives and gives and is never ending.

Love Changes Everything

Healing for everything … for every hurt, every wound, every torment, every betrayal, every loss and every broken heart is there for you, if you want it.

You can choose, He will never force you and manipulate you. What love! He always has open arms for you. He is always accepting and always unconditional.

He is a God of extravagant grace. Just one touch from the King changes everything!

What happens when we experience this kind of love, a supernatural love? It is imprinted into us by heavenly design. It changes everything—especially how we love and view others. The love of God captivates us and we give that love to everyone who needs it (1 John 4:19).

I encourage you today, if you need a safe place, or know someone who does, sit under the shadow of the Almighty's wing and let Him tend your needs, heal and restore you, and let you rest a while. However, beware! Once you are mended, He will then kick you out of the nest like a mother eagle so you can soar into the destiny He created for you even before you were born.

Psalm 16:11 is my favourite Bible verse:

"You will make known to me the path of life,

In Your presence is fullness of joy,

In Your right hand there are pleasures forever."

Let's live the life, display Jesus in everything we do, and attract the favour of heaven around our household. Walk in the fullness God has for you and fly high like an eagle!

Contribution by Annabelle Wallnau

I was born into a very loving family. My parents are still alive and have been married for 59 years.

It's easy for me to smile when I introduce you to them, the Naples Family. I have two brothers, four sisters, and twelve nieces and nephews. We have a love fest whenever we're together.

We are all a product of our environment. In my case, my love of people was primarily cultivated from the earliest experiences of "loving life" with my family.

Secondly, I married Lance Wallnau (an adventure in and of itself) and our families had been friends for a very long time before that. Both our dads served our community together, and so I've known Lance since I was just nine years old.

He and I joke about having an arranged marriage, because his mother didn't really care which daughter married into the family—as long as one of them did! She tried to fix up my oldest sister, Michele, with her oldest son, Carl. When that didn't work out, she tried to connect my older sister, Marie, with Lance! Finally she reached her goal when she invited my father to, "Bring whatever daughters" to their Christmas party on December 18, 1982. I showed up. Lance and I were literally together every day after that until we were married nearly three years later on November 16, 1985.

All these special relationships have caused my love capacity to enlarge. And as if that wasn't enough, we then had three amazing children of our own: Lance Jr., Carl, and Joy. I worked with Lance as a co-pastor in those early days of motherhood, but still had a most wonderful experience of what we fondly refer to as "Raising up Wallnau."

Having children creates training opportunities in noticing "the special moments" and appreciating the unique factor of each person, especially because of how God creates each one so remarkably different.

By becoming intentionally aware of the people in our life and learning to be "present" in the moment—pausing to turn our focus and attention on them and capture the full scope of the moment—we demonstrate how valuable they are to us and this affirms them. Trust is built and genuine rapport is a result. This takes practice, but in time can become second nature. Every relationship in your life will benefit from learning this skill and putting it into regular practice.

I would say that building relationships and bonds of love that cannot be broken are efforts seeded with intentionality from the start. A good friend is always thinking of ways to bless and hold the other person in a place of love. There are times when these ideals get tested and threatened, but time always reveals the heart of the matter.

No matter what the state of your relationships happens to be, know that with attention, they can improve. You can mend and tend and nurture the growth you want to see. All efforts to this end are worthwhile and I encourage you to explore the possibilities that are afforded by cultivating healthy relationships.

Annabelle Wallnau
Vice President, The Lance Learning Group
www.LanceWallnau.com
Fort Worth, Texas, USA

Chapter Eight

Tending Your Time

How many times a day do you find yourself rushing to get things done? Looking over your shoulder at the clock to check the time, rushing to appointments so as not to be late, or even waking up with that feeling of rush ... that you have so much to do? You have a mental list in your head that you haven't even had time to write down. Sound familiar?

Let me ask you, did you laugh when you read this because you recognised yourself?

Time is precious. Every breath is a breath of our life here on earth. Life runs at such a fast pace that we are not even aware of the value of each breath we take.

I travel extensively around the world, and have noticed that it is the same in every country. Everyone is in a rush, panicking to get things done. To be honest, the "To Do" lists each day are completely unrealistic!

My life could be incredibly hectic if I let it! For many years I wore myself out striving to accomplish the maximum number of tasks I could complete in a day, because I thought it showed I was keen, reliable, and coped well. In reality, I was wearing myself out, trying to please the people around me, rather than achieving what was truly important.

Father God showed me that He wanted me to be even more effective, and I could be by concentrating on doing a smaller number of things, but doing them really well.

I knew that my personal time with God had been compromised by my busyness. The thing Father God desired from me, more than anything else, was my full attention. My time, my focus, all of me—and of course that is exactly what I really wanted! Without me even realising, the pressure of life had taken over. I even felt guilty about sitting and doing "nothing" but spending time with my Lord. It just shows you how subtle the deception is!

One day I was sitting in my prayer house and asked God this, "In my busy life of family, church, ministry, work, and looking after the horses, how is it possible to do what You have asked me?"

The answer came back loud and clear, "It is time to draw aside with me, and let some of the things go, even though I know your heart is to bless others."

One by one, I looked at every area of my life. How could I simplify or get help in these areas?

Once I realised that I needed to be single-minded; to rearrange my life to be "available" for an audience of One, things started to fall into place. Even if I travel to speak at a church or fellowship, I now guard my time and tell my hosts in advance that I need my own prayer and rest time in the schedule.

I've had to be more intentional with my time. I've even had to turn down some wonderful opportunities because they would just fill up my time again.

At home I also feel differently about things. I can now enjoy being "at home" without feeling the pressure to get up and do something. I am much more relaxed. (This is especially true after being given a prophetic word at IHOP about being "oh so fussy, wanting everything tidy and just right!")

If you want your time to bear God's fruit, do everything intentionally. Jesus said, "Truly, truly, I say to you, the Son can do nothing of Himself, unless it is something He sees the Father doing" (John 5:19). Slow down, do whatever you need to do to put the One who loves you and desires your time first. Then you will be in a better place to hear the revelation of heaven for yourself, and for those around you. There is a supernatural realm of God's time that is different to earthly time.

If you are too busy to give God that time then something is wrong in your way of living and I encourage you today to start doing something about it today.

Contribution by Gloria Manimuthu

How do we make the best use of time? As seed can be planted, time can be invested and harvested. How you invest your time today determines your future. God has set different seasons for each of our lives. Learn to recognise the season you are in right now. It will enable you to appreciate where you are at, knowing it's not permanent. If I want gorgeous colorful tulips to stand tall in our garden in spring, I have to plant those bulbs in the fall and allow them to be dormant in the winter. I can enjoy the blooms in the spring, but must prune them down in the summer. Time works just like a garden. Prioritize and invest the time for the season you are in right now.

I'm a wife, mom, partner in business, and a student. Chella and I got married after I received my bachelor's degree. I moved from India to the United States because my husband was working there. I was planning to pursue my master's degree after I got acquainted with my new place, the culture, and married life (a newlywed season). During that time God blessed us with our son John, and I became a stay at home mom to invest my time in nurturing God's precious gift to us (a stay-at-home mom season). When John started school, I worked part time in a bank to gain experience in the work field (and enter an employee season). After a year and a half, my employer asked me to work full time. It didn't last more than three weeks because I couldn't fulfill my priority as wife and mom to the level of excellence I am committed to.

After the birth of our second son Joshua, and it was back to the previous (stay-at-home mom) season. When Joshua was a toddler, God burned a desire in Chella to be an entrepreneur. He started an engineering consulting firm in our basement. Being an encourager, supporter, and organizer, I helped him organise and do accounts. The challenge to learn excited me and put me on a path to learn and grow with my husband and our company (a part-owner season).

After helping Chella for nine years, my desire to pursue my graduate degree was kindled in me. I'm currently doing a two year Master's program in Business Administration and at the time I write this contribution, I have just ten months remaining before I finish. Ours boys are now fifteen and ten, and I enjoy driving them for their after school activities and continue to help at the office too (a combination season).

Be and do your very best, no matter what season you are in now. Whatever assignment God has for you at this time in your life, do it unto Him with all your heart, soul, mind, and strength. The return on your investment will depend on the quality of time you invest and not just the quantity. Time is a talent that has been given to you by your Creator. Invest it and multiply it. Dream with your Creator. He invested His time by sending His Son. I encourage you to do the following:

- Invest time in your spouse—be their greatest cheer leader.

- Invest time in your children—nations may be changed by your kid.

- Invest time to pursue your dreams—they will surely come to pass.

- Invest time to lift up and love others—you'll find yourself in places that will amaze you!

Gloria Manimuthu
Treasurer
Cornerstone Engineering, Inc. USA

Chapter Nine

Tending Your Creativity

When I was a little girl, I used to spend a lot of time at Nanny and Grandad's house. They had old apple trees in their garden, and our rope swing hung from the huge branches on the tree in the middle of the garden. My brother Peter, cousin Luke, and I had so much fun in that garden! We were always dressing up: I was Pocahontas (an Indian squaw) and Peter and Luke were always cowboys. I've had an affinity with tribal people as long as I can remember, especially First Nations People. Little did I know that in later life I would be working with them, and even be given an Indian name! It is an honor and pleasure to be part of a prayer network for the Indigenous Tribes of Alaska and around the world.

Almost every time I went to my grandparents' house, I would sit under that old apple tree and meet with my friends, the "fairies." Years later I realised that they were not fairies at all, but my guardian angels and their names are "Glory" and "Grace." I have gotten to know them very well now, but in my younger days they were just fairies! (I am not talking about the Tinker Bell Type of fairy—mine were huge!)

Glory and Grace took me on journeys to many lands and I met many different looking people. I remember my first encounter with a Lion that I grew to know as Aslan!

It was only many years later, after I read the Narnia stories, that I remembered I had seen that lamp post before!

I flew on eagles' wings with Glory and Grace by my side and I had many personal experiences that are for my heart only, never to be spoken about. To me it was a very normal thing to be doing.

At school I used to get into trouble for "daydreaming" and being "dramatic" as I acted out my experiences pretending to "fly" in the playground! No one believed me and my teacher used to shake her head and say I was, "Away with the fairies" … little did they know I really was!

My teachers used to tell me I was imagining things. I had to stand crying in the corner of the classroom many times because no one would believe me. Slowly, slowly, my imagination was shut down—colours were not so vibrant anymore, and I stopped seeing Glory and Grace.

The educational system suggested to my parents that instead of going into a mainstream secondary school, I should go to an art and drama school. I was accepted into The Arts Education School, Tring, Hertfordshire, UK, where they actively encouraged people to express their natural talents—art, drama, dance, and imagination! Through my training there I had the opportunity to take part in many TV series and films, which was a great way to use the talents God gave me. I have my parents to thank for their openness to allow me to be me, and for sending me to this very expensive school at great sacrifice to themselves.

When I became a Christian I had a problem: the church loved me and we had fabulous times together, but I never really fitted in! They did not understand me, and they did a good job at trying to mold me into someone I was not.

Thank goodness I was rescued by Father God Himself, who showed me that He made me who I am! He loves my passion for Him and my heart. The reason I am sharing these most private things is because I care so much about YOU being released to be the person God made you to be. My desire is that if you have experienced being shut down, bound up, or made to be someone you are not, that just by reading this, you will dare to move into a realm of heavenly glory, light and colour! I pray that you will have an encounter with your guardian angels ... or even better, with Father God Himself!

We must be so careful not to judge and close down people just because they are not the same as us. I am sure many of you have received either a critical word, or a word that pieced your heart—a word that closed down something creative that God put inside of you, because you did not conform to the "box" of their understanding. I would ask all teachers to be very sensitive to each individual child. Let them dream and soar with angels.

Many years later, married with children of my own, I had a life-changing encounter with the Holy Spirit. My friend Loraine and I had gone to a church meeting, just out of interest really, as some friends had just returned from the revival outpouring at Toronto. Our intention was only to observe, but as we stood with everyone, I was hit by a flame of fire that came straight out of heaven. My whole body felt like it was burning, my feet especially, and I ended up hopping around the room laughing and laughing and everyone I touched caught the fire. I was like this for a few weeks. I worked for the Walt Disney group at this time, and every light switch and cash register I touched would blow up ... until they told me not to touch anything at all! Such was the power running through me. When it happens now, I warn people to not get too close as I know what will happen! I can't explain it any other way as there is no earthly explanation to it! My spiritual eyes opened to see into the spirit, and then I realised Glory and Grace had never left me, I just could not see them. I had only seen them in the natural as a child, but I began to see them in their true supernatural form.

While pregnant with our fourth child, I had gone strawberry picking with a friend. I ate as many strawberries as I picked to be honest! I was kneeling down looking for the juiciest strawberries when feathers brushed past my face and I was overwhelmed with the presence of love. I recognised whose feathers they were. I cried at the joy of reconnection with my angels, but I never said anything to my friend. It was simply too personal. When I got home Martin, my husband, had left a note on our kitchen table that said, "Did you feel the angels wings brush past you today?" Umm, how did he know that, I wonder?

What did I learn that day? I learned to always be expectant for the touch of Heaven.

Do you realise that there is a creative spark inside of you that is just waiting to be released?

Genesis 1:26-27 tells us how God created man in His image.

"Then God said, 'Let us make man in Our image, according to Our likeness: let them have dominion over the fish of the sea, and over the birds of the sky and over cattle and over all the earth, and over every creeping thing that creeps on the earth.' God created man in His Own image, in the image of God He created him, male and female, He created them."

When we are creating we are releasing that image. It is a grace manifestation.

Whether it is art or music or a technical innovation of a business process, open your spirit and reach for the heavenly perspective. You may experience insight through a word of knowledge or a word of wisdom (1 Corinthians 12:8), or a revelation of a heavenly pattern to be reproduced on earth (Hebrew 8:4-5), but however it comes you will be bearing spiritual fruit.

Jesus said, "My Father is glorified by this, that you bear much fruit, and so prove to be My disciples" (John 15:8). I believe that you will bring glory to the Father as you do!

Right now I speak life, wholeness, and creativity to be released in you. Enjoy the journey, but don't expect everyone to understand you ... how could they as you are now moving in a different realm!

Contribution Amy Reynolds-Corden

Creativity, if I'm honest, is a word that I have often struggled with. I have sometimes found it hard to understand why some people are defined as "creative" or more "creative" than others, because I believe that everyone has the potential to be creative, whether they are aware of it or not. I come from a very musical family and have grown up surrounded by music in any and every form, but I'm not sure there was a moment in my life where I suddenly realised that I was musically "creative." It has been something that God has continued to reveal to me and release in me as I journey with Him and seek to know Him more.

Nevertheless, there was one specific moment in my life when God spoke to me so powerfully and creatively that I continue to be blown away in awe and wonder every time I think about it. I can't remember exactly when it was, but I know that I was only seven or eight years old. Just before this experience, when I was just six, my dad walked out on my mum, my brother and I and I remember being very angry at God for allowing the breakup of our family.

One morning I woke up, pulled back the curtains and looked out of the window. What I saw will stay with me for the rest of my life. The sun was rising and the sky was ablaze with colours of blue, pink, yellow, silver, and gold. It was the most glorious thing I have ever seen. But there was more. The clouds had formed the most incredible landscape I had ever seen, stretching across the entire horizon for as far as I could see. There were hills and valleys, rivers and fields, oceans, islands, beaches, and bays that stretched out across the sky.

At that moment I knew that God was showing me just the tiniest glimpse of heaven—that He was my perfect heavenly Father who loved me unconditionally. He was showing me that he hadn't abandoned me or my family, and that there was a place for me in heaven one day.

However, growing up and into my late teenage years and my early twenties, I continued to judge myself according to the world. I told myself that I couldn't possibly be "creative" because I wasn't an incredible artist or painter, I couldn't write a hit song (pop or worship) in ten minutes flat. I didn't play eight different instruments, and I couldn't sing like Whitney Houston. I was never cut out to be a worship leader (even though deep down I knew that was the calling God had placed on my life) because I simply wasn't good enough.

Yet God in His infinite mercy, love, and grace, continued to pursue me and encourage the dreams He had placed in my heart, even though I tried to run from them and suppress them. It is a journey I am still very much on. It has only been in the last eighteen months that I have truly stepped up into the calling that God has for my life as a musician and worship leader. I still struggle with doubts and the comparisons I make between myself and other people, but I have learned something very important that I would love to share with you.

I am at my most creative when I do
exactly what I was created to do in the first place.

John Piper wrote that "God is most glorified in us, when we are most satisfied in Him." My creativity flows when I reach that place of total surrender to God, when I lay everything down that would hinder me from coming into His presence, and when I step into the calling that God has on my life. I do not reach the pinnacle of my creativity when I write a fantastic lyric, or play a piece of music to the very best of my ability. Instead, for me personally, I am most creative when I stand up and lead people into His presence through music and worship. When I allow the Holy Spirit to release creativity in me, not only am I reflecting God's creativity, I am reflecting His glory.

Every single one of us is creative. We are all created in the image of a creative God. It can be so easy to define creativity by worldly standards and therefore, pigeonhole ourselves as "uncreative" because our God-given creativity does not fit into the box that is of this world labelled "creative." This causes us to shrink away from our creative gifts because we are so blinkered by what the world demands of us, that if our creativity doesn't fit, then surely we weren't creative in the first place!

My encouragement to you is this. Dare to dream. Release your imagination. Surrender all of yourself to the Lord. Allow Him to work in and through you. Be bold enough to step out in faith into the calling He has placed on your life.

The God who is able to do immeasurably more than you could ever ask or imagine is the God who knit you together while you were in your mother's womb and who, through the power of His Holy Spirit working in your life, longs to see you fulfill your creative potential in Him.

———————————————

Amy Reynolds-Corden
Discipleship Training Year and Worship Internship
at St. Thomas Crookes
Sheffield, UK

Chapter Ten

Tending Your Storehouse

Being at the farm every day and working with animals has taught me that you have to plan ahead. Not only do you have to plan the times you feed, muck out the stables, clean the yard, and hay the horses, but you also have to buy (ahead of time) the provisions you will need for the following months. If you do not, and there is a shortage because of extreme weather conditions or a problem with supplies, not only will you run out of the essential things you need, but even if you can find them, they are overly expensive as suppliers exploit the situation and increase their prices.

You also have to plan the rotation of the fields so that they can be rested to stop overgrazing, and new grass can be given a chance to grow. You must plan what fields will be used to grow hay for the following year, and when the hay will be harvested, baled, and stored.

You must even plan which barn will hold hay, straw, feed, etc. This must be sorted out in advance. Without planning, a farm could not run efficiently—no food would be stored for the difficult winter season. A barn with a leaky roof could ruin a whole year's hay supply and grain harvest at great expense. The loss could also end up with starving animals.

The same principle of planning applies to the water supply: no water, no life. Pipes and taps need to be maintained well so that they don't freeze over, snap, or leak. Also, to waste water when the water is metered is very costly.

The same applies to the financial running of a farm: you have to be able to provide the equipment and machinery needed to feed the animals and care for the fields. If they do not plan their finances to be able to do these things, farmers will have a stressful life, and perhaps not even be able to survive difficult economic times.

I read Al Jandl's book called *The Storehouse Principle* last year. In this book Al takes us back to the Old Testament to look at what God says about "storehouses," and the command of Christ to be a good steward in all areas of your life, especially in the area of finances.

To provide for a sound financial footing, it is also necessary to tithe. In fact, tithing actually releases the blessings to us! Deuteronomy 28:8 holds this amazing promise:

Tending Your Storehouse

"The Lord will command the blessings on
you in your storehouses and in all to which
you set your hand, and He will bless you in
the land your God is giving you."

Father God has given us a revolutionary way to have
financial security and all the provisions we need for
our families and our children's children. Deuteronomy
8:18 says this:

"And you shall remember the Lord your God,
for it is He who gives you power to get wealth,
that He may establish His covenant which He
swore to your fathers, as it is this day."

Who's strategy do you use to plan your finances?
Is it the bank's strategy, something you learned in an
investment magazine, or the Word of God?

I have always trusted God for provision, and He has
always been faithful. At times our family has walked
through difficulties, learning how to become good
stewards of our finances. It has taken me a long time to
learn to live within our means—partly because I was not
used to working within a budget, but mostly because
I love to bless others and wanted to help anyone who
had a need, even beyond what we had available to give!

We have always tithed, and God has blessed us. As
I grew in God, I believe He was teaching me a lesson,
to not only be a good steward with our tithes and
offerings, but also to become a good steward of our
day-to-day finances.

We are a family that requires two incomes to make ends meet each month. When I left my job to pursue unpaid full-time ministry, our finances suffered for several years, despite being helped out by family and friends.

One morning we received a letter from our bank that really frightened me. It said that if we could not immediately make a deposit, our account would be frozen. How would we buy food, run the car, or pay the house mortgage? I had an unction from the Lord to go straight down to the bank, not realising you have to make an appointment to see the manager. I had no idea what I was going to do to get out of this situation. We had asked God to help, hoping money would fall from Heaven, but instead He sent me to the bank manager!

I'm so glad He did, because I was seen straight away, given a cup of tea, and simply explained our situation and asked her, "What would you suggest?"

Within an hour I came out so excited! She worked out a wonderful action plan that gave us hope, reduced some payments with just a phone call, and set up a "storehouse" account in which we put £1 (the first fruit)! Suddenly I was able to look at things differently. Even though this lady was a Hindu, God met us both in that room. He explained to me the provision around me to make wealth, and she got a word from God for her personal situation. When I left, the bank manager gave me a big hug and cried. I had gone there to get her help, and she had gotten mine as well!

I realised that as I was a good steward of the small things, God could entrust me with more—even in the financial realm.

As I am thanking God for what He has taught me in this area, I would also thank my good friends Tracy and Ana Bennett, who have modeled financial stewardship to me.

At Lance Wallnau's "Train The Trainer" event in Texas, I had an "Ah-ha" moment. I realised that my intercessory ministry was of eternal value, and that it was not wrong to be paid for the time I spent labouring on other's behalf. (This is similar to the principle found in Galatians 6:6, pertaining to Bible teachers.)

I have experienced such a turnaround in just a few short years!

Once I aligned myself to heaven's perspective on money, it released a blessing not only on my family, but also in the lives of those around me.

The storehouse principle doesn't just apply to finances, but also to resources such as time, relationships, and the abilities that God entrusts us with.

I so wish that I had had this revelation sooner, and I passionately share it with anyone who will listen and have a positive change in their life!

Contribution by Tory L. McJunkin

I'm different. I come from old money. I come from a wealthy family—a very wealthy family. We live in the big house ...the really BIG house with the security gates, the long cobblestone driveway, the fountains, the pools, the stables, the garages, the heli-pad, the lush finely manicured lawns, and the amazing views. The house itself is intricate and beautiful. It's crafted with the finest materials and uses the best of everything. It has imports from all around the world: Tuscan marble, hand-carved Indian beamed ceilings, encrusted jewels, gold leafing, custom fireplaces and balustrades, and original artwork. Every room has a purpose and a view.

Our property is home for me, but if you haven't been to a house like this, it's hard to describe. I guess a house like this is called extravagant, and isn't necessary, but what is necessary? Is beauty? Is music? Is the ocean? Are the mountains?

I do have one little secret ... I'm adopted. This is my Father's house, but I get to live here! My Father is a God of abundance. He is lavish. He is beautiful. He is a wild lover. He is an amazing creator. We are going to a place with streets and even buildings made of gold. Gates are made of single pearls, and walls are made of every kind of precious stone. We are going to a place that is indescribable and awe inspiring ... if we love and accept Jesus.

God has given each of us an incredible and mind-blowing new family. He has also given us the capacity to love, to choose, and to serve. We were designed to use and multiply (think logarithmic) the gifts and talents that God has given each one of us. We are also called to live with wisdom and discernment in all areas of our lives. As members of society we have mortgages to pay, a continuous stream of bills, and mouths to feed every day. Finances and how we earn them, spend them, save them or don't save them, take up an incredible part of our daily lives. Finances also play a large part in our most important relationships and many experts believe the number one reason that marriages end in divorce is because of money problems.

Finances are often relegated to the practical, necessary, and even important category, but are often considered non-spiritual or worse yet, anti-spiritual. We live in a society that idolizes greed, readily accepts debt, and approves of materialism. It's not hard for us to fall into the trap that finances and any attention to them is worldly and underserving of our time or resources. Unfortunately, this is unbiblical, naïve, and simply untrue. Regarding our finances, we are called to so much more than worldly standards. We are called to a much higher standard called Kingdom living.

Kingdom living is incredible and is very different than earthly wisdom. It requires principals set in motion and designed by the King; our Designer, and the Creator of all. "The Lord will command the blessing on you in your storehouses and in all to which you set your hand and He will bless you in the land which the Lord your God is giving you" (Deuteronomy 28:8).

From this verse we can see that we are called to "set our hands" to things: our work, inventions, tinkering, repairs, building plans, and so on. We are further instructed, "Whatever you do, work at it with all your heart, as working for the Lord, not for human masters" (Colossians 3:23). We are also called to have "storehouses" and to allow God to bless them. Even ants (and squirrels) have storehouses. "Go to the ant, you sluggard! Consider her ways and be wise" (Proverbs 6:6). We also see from this verse that there is "land" or territory that the "Lord our God is giving us."

I hope you can see having storehouses requires monitoring, planning, and increasing our finances with God's help. Tending our storehouses is a kingdom principal that requires several things. Most importantly we have to know the King to understand His principals. (God goes one step further by allowing the Holy Spirit to reside and rule in each of us). Remember "my" house of abundance and my extravagant Father? That is the God that we serve. We are adopted by the King with the BIG house!

Remember Joseph and the massive life-saving storehouses that he created? Joseph saved countries (Egypt and Israel) because of his obedience to God's calling on his life. He was a man who worked hard with excellence. "Do you see someone skilled in their work? They will serve before kings" (Proverbs 22:29).

Ultimately everything that we have is from and for Jesus. Jesus paid the ultimate sacrifice to redeem every aspect of you for His kingdom. "'Bring all the tithes into the storehouse, that there may be food in My house, *and try Me now in this*,' Says the Lord of hosts, 'If I will not open for you the windows of heaven And pour out for you such blessing that there will not be room enough to receive it'" (Malachi 3:10, author's emphasis).

Our God of abundance says, "And try Me now in this." The first thing we need to do is allow the Holy Spirit to change our minds to one of abundance, which enables us to obey. God is so BIG. His ways are so much higher than ours. The universe is so huge and He simply spoke it into existence. God is crazy. He is huge. He is scary awesome.

The second is an action step: we must tithe. I repeat, we must tithe. If you don't (or have never been taught to) tithe or give your first fruits, understand that God can't bless you in the way that He wants to. God is waiting to "open up the windows of heaven and pour out for you such blessing that there will not be room enough to receive it." I'll make you a deal. If you tithe and God doesn't come through, contact me ... I'll reimburse you for your troubles.

Finally, we are called to be good stewards. The Bible is clear that we don't own anything, we are only watching over God's things. We are called to grow them and to give those things that God has given us (our kids, our money, our house, our ministries, our success, etc.). In the end, everything that we have is a gift from God. The Bible is pretty clear, we are to give to those in need. We are to support the orphans and widows. We are to live in community and share our blessings with those who have need. We are to use our money to bless missionaries, ministries, and practically spread the good news. We are to use our money shrewdly and even to store up money for future generations. Whenever the process has been completed, then the process starts over again.

○ Renew your mind

○ Tithe

○ Be a good steward

This process gives me so much joy. I love making money (it's all from Him). I love saving money (it's all for Him). I love tithing and sharing God's great abundance with others ("blessing someone's socks off"). I love being a good steward. God calls us to tend our financial storehouses and to grow them. By God's grace, I'm growing my storehouses. You can too.

Tory L. McJunkin, M.D., D.A.B.A.
Founder, Arizon Pain Specialists
Arizona, USA

Part Three

The Blessings From Your Garden

Tending Your Garden

Chapter Eleven

Enjoying Your Garden

Picture a perfect summer's day. The gardening is done. All the plants have been watered and the tools put away. It's time to get out the patio chairs, plump up the cushions, and put the sunshade on the table. Slip off your sandals, climb on the chair, and "Ahhhh!" Time to relax!

When God created the world, did He not say, "... and on the seventh day, He rested"?

Last year I realised that, with conference calls in so many different time zones, the length of my working week had almost doubled, and that I was actually having no free time at all.

On a ministry trip to Alaska in May 2012, Father God surprised me and renewed a deep desire in my heart. It was at the end of the trip that my dear friend Barb decided to take me to see a display of Western riding. I enjoy the work of ministry, but was so looking forward to this treat.

As we sat to watch the display, instead of western riding, we were presented with a "horses from around the world" display.

The first horse to enter the arena was a huge, beautiful, black Friesian from Holland. On top of this magnificent, gentle giant sat a six or seven year old girl and they did a beautiful riding display.

"Boom!" In my ear I heard Father God say, "You will have a horse like this within a month." I had never thought of having such a big horse or even a black horse, but sure enough God was faithful to His word. Within two weeks of me being back home, my Mr. Darcy came into my life, through a set of events that only God could orchestrate!

He is my relaxation, but also provides me with times to enjoy wonderful communion with God.

Dare to believe that God will give you the desires of your heart too, even if you do not understand them yourself.

If you have diligently tended your garden, there is a time of rest for you. You are ready to move from the hard work of preparation to the being—living in a place where heaven is open to you because there are no hindrances in the way of interacting with heaven.

You are now ready to explore "Experiential Intercession" ... and we will talk more about this in my next book!

Contribution by Yvonne Cooke

In You I live and move and have my being
My senses are heightened to your creation
Through the lens of perfect love.

The songbird awakens the day, singing
Bringing life, declaration
Of today, and all that is good.

In my garden nature is screaming
Poppies stand guard in a red standing ovation
As a fly-past of white clouds circle above.

A raindrop holds fast to a sticky leaf, glistening,
With a transparent testimony of elation
At it's flawless form. Water of life.

The spider's web shyly shimmering
Awash with dew, a hanging suspension,
A delicate trap for a far from focussed fly.

All of a sudden, the noise of children fills my ears
A memory floods back from distant years
A slide, a hose pipe, a watery descent
Down the garden hours of fun spent.
Slipping and sliding, laughing and shrieking
Till bedtime beckons,
Bathtime done outside on the lawn
Little faces wanting, "More, Mum, more!"

Garden left soaking in puddles galore
Siblings all sleeping, one or two gently snore.
I hang out their costumes to dry overnight
Ready for the morning, poised for sunlight.
My garden overflows now and then with delight.
Oh we are so precious in His sight.

Evening approaches, a fragrance is wafting
On the gentle evening breeze, affirmation
That the honeysuckle is alive.

Sunset reddens the sky, heralding
The promise of a new morning, anticipation
Of something more from my God.

I taste and I see, drinking
In the sounds of the evening, celebration
Enjoying my garden and all that is mine.

Yvonne Cooke
Intercessor & Worship Leader, UK

Contribution by Una Gere

Butterflies have always attracted me, and have played an important part in my life since early childhood. When I was just six or seven years old, my God-mother brought me a marzipan butterfly from

Paris. This began a love for the beautiful creatures, and I was later touched by a butterfly "angel" the Lord sent to me during one of the most scary, faith-stretching moments of my life!

When I was a child, I loved to watch and chase butterflies. There were different kinds to be found in all the different seasons. From the white-ish cabbage butterflies of spring, to the orange and brown and speckled varieties of summer, all were gorgeous. All were unique. I loved to watch them pick up the pollen from the garden flowers, even as they sipped their nectar, before flitting off to deposit that same pollen elsewhere. They were busy, but always graceful, always at peace.

Later I learned about the great diversity of butterflies, their unique habits, habitats, and lifespans. I even heard about a phenomenon called the "butterfly effect," where one butterfly, by simply moving its wings, can affect weather patterns that can cause a tsunami on the other side of the world. This has been proven scientifically and shows how even the smallest of events can have enormous repercussions. The implications are amazing!

As an adult, I have loved visiting butterfly farms from Switzerland to Malaysia, and never fail to be in awe of their beauty and grace.

I heard this whisper early one morning, "You are not a caterpillar. You are a butterfly." In my heart, I asked, "Lord, what do you mean?"

I felt Him answer, "Stop eating caterpillar food. Sip the nectar I provide through My Word and through My other beautiful butterflies. Stop clunking around on your caterpillar feet, chomping on the things of this world. It's time to soar, to flit "lightly and freely" (Matthew 11:28-30; Revelation 4:1). There is a call to "set our minds on things above" (Colossians 3:1-2), and not dwell on the bad news of this world. "Be ye transformed," says Paul (Romans 12:1-2). Put another way, be "metamorphosed" from caterpillar to butterfly.

The Lord went on to say, "I was the first butterfly. I went into the tomb (cocoon) as a man (caterpillar), and emerged as a new, transformed, metamorphosed creation. And so you, in Me, are that new, beautiful creation butterfly.

I must confess that when I look into the mirror, I most often still see a caterpillar; but I KNOW that I am a butterfly. I am determined to live the best butterfly life I can. I will fulfill His earthly plan for me—to live gloriously, radically, freely, as that one who has inherited this new life. Hallelujah! I want to encourage all you who have found your way to the garden. Keep exhorting others, calling out and adorning the other beautiful butterflies around you. Help those around you to see how very beautiful, amazing, and significant they are. As we each come and meet the Gardener, who loves and tends His garden so very well, we are being "transformed" into His likeness, "from glory to glory" (Corinthians 3:17).

Enjoying Your Garden

The Gardener, it's all about Him. His call, His song to us is "Come, come, arise and come. If you are hungry, thirsty, weary, burdened, come. Respond to My call."

"I am the way, the truth, the life—the only way.
I am Abba—so come."
Matthew 11:28 (MSG)

Una Gere
Leadership Team of Succat Hallel, HOP
Jerusalem, Israel

"Show me your garden and I shall tell you what you are."

Alfred Austin
English Poet Laureate

Made in the USA
Coppell, TX
21 June 2022

79083713R00070